Make Your Own Presents

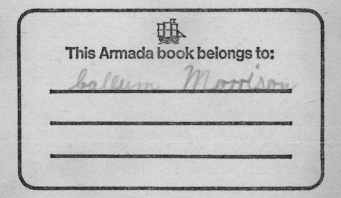

This Armada book belongs to:

Callum Morrison

Hal Danby is a design consultant and inventor, and one-time television floor manager and racing driver. He is the author of Car Quiz, also an Armada book, and he and his wife live in Essex with a dog called Barkis and a cat called Valentine.

Make Your Own Presents

HAL DANBY

illustrated by Bernard Taylor

Armada

Make Your Own Presents
was first published in the U.K. in 1974
by William Collins Sons & Co Ltd
14 St James's Place, London SW1

© Hal Danby 1974

Printed in Great Britain by
William Collins Sons & Co Ltd,
London & Glasgow

Contents

Introduction

Make Your Own Presents contains many varied items ranging in difficulty and cost. Most of the presents are easily made from materials which can be found about the house.

Each page is headed with a list of the required materials, and any special tools that may be required. It has been assumed that most households have a simple selection of small tools.

WARNING
PAINT CAN BE DANGEROUS

Most household paint contains poisonous lead. This type of paint, even when dry, can be dangerous – or even fatal – if eaten or sucked by a small child.

Please, where possible, use lead-free enamels which can be bought from craft or model shops. The Humbrol or Joy ranges are ideal.

Do's and Don'ts

PAINTING

DO:

Sandpaper the article smooth before starting.

Fill any cracks with plaster filler.

Apply wood primer to bare wood.

Use undercoat before the final gloss coat.

Stir the paint well.

DON'T:

Paint on top of dirt or dust.

Apply the next coat until the previous one is dry.

Put on too much paint at a time.

NAILING

DO:

Choose the right nails for the job.

Draw a line for the nails when working along an edge.

DON'T:

Use rusty or bent nails.

Spoil the wood with hammer marks.

Use a large nail near an edge. This could split the wood.

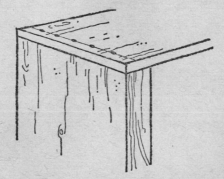

Draw a straight line for the nails

SAWING

DO:

Use the correct saw for the job.

Cut just to one side of a marked line.

Go carefully towards the end of a cut to stop the wood splitting.

DON'T:

Use a broken or blunt saw.

Saw wood which is not held firmly.

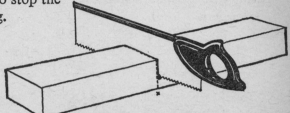

Saw just to one side of a marked line

CUTTING

DO:

Use a really sharp knife— this is safer than a blunt one.

Use a straight edge where possible.

DON'T:

Place your fingers in front of the blade.

Cut anything which is not firmly held.

Cut along a straight edge

GLUEING

DO:

Follow the instructions carefully.

Allow plenty of time to dry.

Hold the glued articles together where possible, using elastic bands, clamps or weights.

DON'T:

Glue on to dirty surfaces.

Hold glued articles together firmly

Wall tidy

1 Cut a piece of cloth slightly larger than the wall tidy that you want to make.

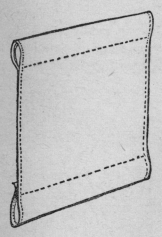

2 Hem the sides and make extra wide hems at the top and bottom. (These should be wide enough to allow the dowelling to slide through them.)

3 Cut one dowel the same width as the wall tidy and the other 5 cms (2 ins) longer. Smooth the ends of the dowels with sandpaper.

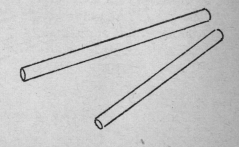

4 Embroider a piece of cloth and sew it along the bottom to form pockets.

5 Make loops for scissors, etc. and sew on bulldog clips for papers, etc.

6 The screw eyes are attached to the wall, and the ends of the top dowel are passed through them.

Cot or pram toy

YOU WILL NEED
Scraps of wool
Thin elastic

SPECIAL EQUIPMENT
None

Please make sure that anything given to a baby is first shown to its parents.

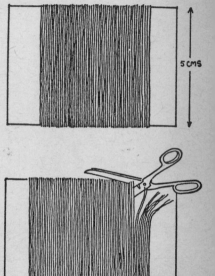

1 Wind the wool around a strip of card 5 cms (2 ins) wide, for about one hundred turns.

5 CMS

2 With a pair of scissors, cut through the woollen strands along one edge of the card, so that you are left with a bundle of 10 cm lengths of wool. This process may have to be repeated until you have enough bundles to make the required number of "men".

3 Tie a piece of wool around each bundle near one end. Repeat this process slightly further down each bundle to form the head. The face can be decorated with either coloured wool or cotton.

4 Separate twenty strands from
each side of the bundles to
form the arms, cut 2½ cms
(1 in) off each arm and tie
wool around the end of
each.

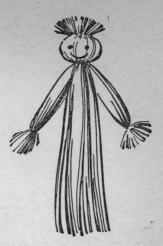

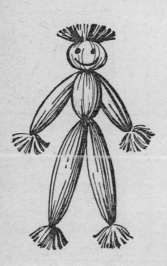

5 Tie wool around the waist,
and separate the bundle in
half to form the legs.
Finally, tie the bottom of
each leg.

6 Thread some fine elastic through each arm so that all the
"men" are suspended arm to arm. Leave enough elastic
on each for tying to the cot or pram.

Table napkins

YOU WILL NEED
Loosely-woven material
Coloured threads

SPECIAL EQUIPMENT
None

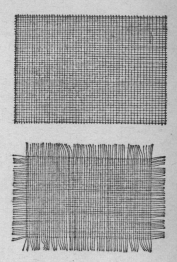

1 Cut a piece of loosely-woven material to the size of a napkin. Make sure that you cut along the grain of the material.

2 Pull out several threads from the four sides, leaving a deep frayed edge.

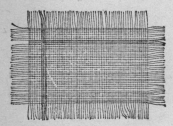

3 Pull out further threads to form a pattern. These can be replaced with contrasting colours of sewing or embroidery silk by weaving them into place.

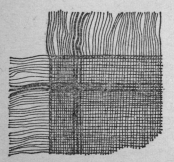

4 To stop further fraying, bind the edges. Do this either with a zig-zag stitch on a sewing machine or by over-stitching.

16

Book mark

YOU WILL NEED
Scraps of clear stiff plastic
Enamel paints

SPECIAL EQUIPMENT
None

1 Cut out the required shape from a sheet of clear plastic. This type of plastic is often used in packaging or can be bought from a model shop.

2 Draw your design in reverse on a piece of paper and attach the plastic to it with small pieces of sticky tape.

3 Paint the design (which will then show through from the other side) on to the plastic, remove your original drawing, and then cover the back of the book mark with two coats of a single colour. This will form the background to your design.

Notice board

YOU WILL NEED
A piece of cork or softboard
A square of baize, felt,
or hessian
Fabric glue (such as Copydex)
Scraps of cloth tape or ribbon

SPECIAL EQUIPMENT
A fine tooth saw (such as a
tenon saw)

The notice board may be used for recipes, photographs, memos, press cuttings, etc.

1 Cut a piece of cork sheeting (or softboard) the size that you want the notice board to be.

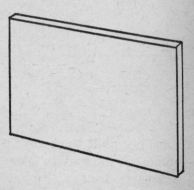

2 Smooth the edges with sandpaper, being careful not to round off the corners.

3 Cut the baize (or felt) 5 cms (2½ ins) larger all around than the cork.

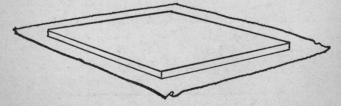

4 Apply glue sparingly to one side of the cork, and place the baize on it, making sure that it is taut, and allowing the same border all around.

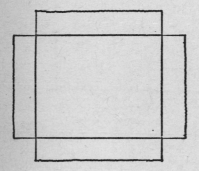

5 Turn the notice board on to its face and cut the baize as shown. Glue one side over at a time, making sure that the corners are neat. The baize will overlap at each corner.

6 Glue two folded strips of ribbon on the back to take a hanging string.

Papier maché jar

YOU WILL NEED
Enamel paints
Wallpaper paste
jam jar
cooking foil
paper

SPECIAL EQUIPMENT
None

1 Cover the outside of a jam jar with cooking foil and smooth it out as much as possible.

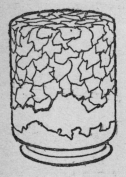

2 Paste small pieces of paper all over the base and down the sides. Repeat this process until five or six layers have been built up.

3 When thoroughly dry, remove the paper shell from the jar and discard the foil.

4 Trim around the top of the jar with a sharp knife or a pair of scissors. To strengthen the edge, more paper strips can be glued over it.

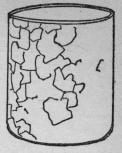

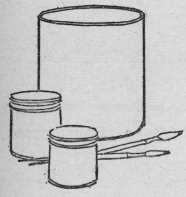

5 Give the jar a coat of undercoat or emulsion, followed by two coats of coloured enamel.

6 Paint on the design of your choice with enamel.

This may be used for sweets or pencils, or even as a flower-pot holder.

Garden tool rack

YOU WILL NEED
A strip of wood
Dowelling
Wood glue

SPECIAL EQUIPMENT
Saw
Drill

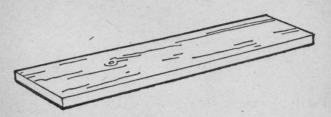

1 Cut a length of wood 10 cms (4 ins) wide by at least 18 mm ($\frac{3}{4}$ in) thick. The length depends on the size of the hanging space.

2 Cut the dowelling into 10 cm (4 in) lengths and round one end of each with sandpaper. The dowelling must be at least 12 mm ($\frac{1}{2}$ in) in diameter.

3 Mark a centre line down the middle of the strip of wood and drill holes exactly the same diameter as the dowelling in the wood at 10 cm (4 in) intervals.

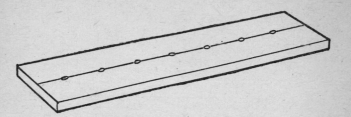

4 Glue the dowels firmly in place in the holes.

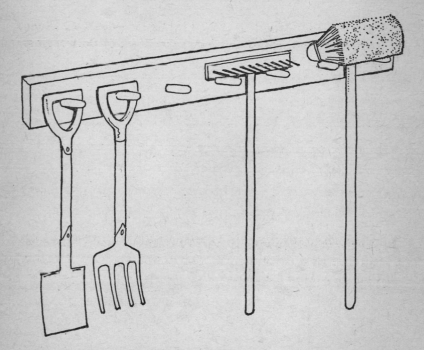

Car stopper

YOU WILL NEED
2½ ozs wool
String

SPECIAL EQUIPMENT
None

Hang the woollen ball in the garage so that it just touches the windscreen when the garage doors can be closed behind the car.

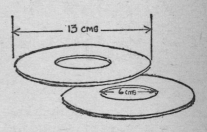

1 Cut two discs of cardboard measuring 13 cms (5 ins) across with a centre hole of 6 cms (2½ ins).

2 Put the two discs together and wind wool round and round them.

3 Continue winding the wool until the centre is completely filled. A large needle might help towards the end.

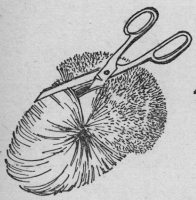

4 Using a sharp knife or scissors, cut the wool around the edge of the cardboard discs.

5 With a piece of light string, tie a tight knot around the wool between the two discs, leaving a long end of string. Cut the two discs away and the ball is complete.

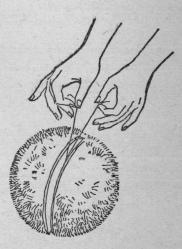

A lamp...

YOU WILL NEED
An attractive bottle
Small piece of felt
Vermiculite (bought from a
garden equipment supplier)
Bulb holder (lamp adaptor)

SPECIAL EQUIPMENT
None

1 Wash the label off the bottle and fill it up to the neck with Vermiculite.

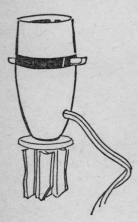

2 Press the bulb holder firmly into the neck.

3 Cover the base with a small piece of felt.

...and a lampshade

YOU WILL NEED
A cheap plain lampshade
Bottle labels
Wallpaper paste

SPECIAL EQUIPMENT
None

1 Carefully soak off labels
from empty bottles.

2 When dry, paste them neatly
over the lampshade.

Gardening apron

YOU WILL NEED
Heavy cloth material
  80 × 92 cms (30 × 36 ins)
A sheet of PVC
  68 × 18 cms (25 × 7 ins)
Four poppers (press studs)

SPECIAL EQUIPMENT
A sewing machine if possible

This gardening apron has a waterproof kneeler which can be let down. The dimensions given would make it suitable for an adult.

1 Cut one piece of material 68 cms (25 ins) square, and another 29 cms (11½ ins) × 24 cms (9½ ins). Hem the first on three sides and the second on one long side and the two short sides.

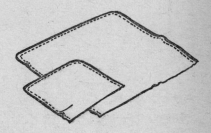

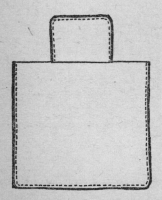

2 Sew the unhemmed edge of the small piece to the middle of the unhemmed side of the large piece.

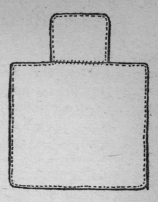

3 Hem the remaining portions of the large piece.

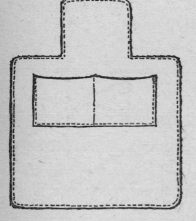

4 Attach a pocket 20 cms (7$\frac{1}{2}$ ins) × 40 cms (15 ins) to the front, about 10 cms (4 ins) below the bib.

5 Sew a patch of PVC 68 cms (25 ins) × 18 cms (7 ins) to the front as shown.

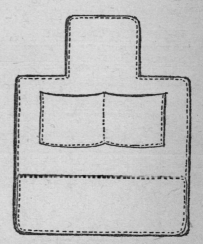

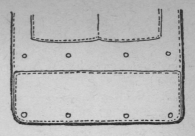

6 The poppers are sewn along the bottom of the PVC-covered area and their other halves along a line just under the pocket.

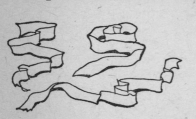

7 Cut 3 pieces of material 42 cms (15 ins) long and 3 cms (1½ ins) wide and hem the edges.

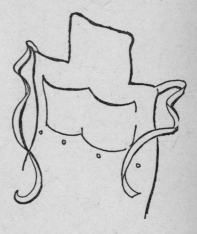

8 Attach two of these tapes to either side of the apron skirt as shown.

9 Attach the ends of the third tape to either side of the bib. If the apron is for a man, this tape should be about 10 cms (4 ins) longer.

Wig or hat stand

YOU WILL NEED
A balloon
Washing-up liquid bottle
Scraps of cloth
Wallpaper paste
Ping-pong ball
Enamel paints

SPECIAL EQUIPMENT
None

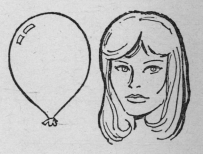

1 Blow up a balloon to the size of a human head.

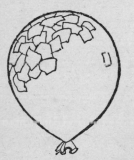

2 Using the wallpaper paste, cover the balloon by pasting on pieces of newspaper not bigger than 2 cms ($\frac{3}{4}$ in) square.

3 Build up at least five layers, leaving the neck of the balloon exposed.

4 When the layers are thoroughly dry and hard, stick a small piece of Sellotape on the neck of the balloon, and pierce the balloon through it with a pin. Remove the balloon from the shell.

5 Cut the top off a washing-up liquid bottle and fill it half full of pebbles. Wedge the pebbles firmly in place with pieces of rolled-up newspaper.

6 Cover the bottle with three layers of paper and sit the neck of the balloon shell in the top.

7 Attach the head to the neck with thin strips of newspaper pasted into place. Stick five layers of paper over the join.

8 When the whole assembly
is thoroughly dry and hard,
paint it with undercoat or
white emulsion. Follow
this with two coats of
white enamel.

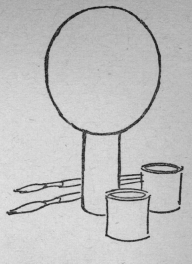

9 Paint the ping-pong ball
bright red and glue it
firmly in place as the nose.

10 Finally paint the wig stand
with enamel paints to look
like a clown.

Sewing jar
with pin-cushion lid

YOU WILL NEED
An empty coffee jar
Some pieces of felt
A length of braid
Suitable fabric glue
Some scraps of foam

SPECIAL EQUIPMENT
None

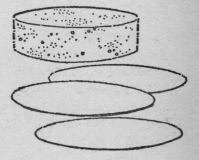

1 Cut out some foam 4 cms
(1½ ins) thick, the same
diameter as the lid of the
coffee jar. Also cut out
three circles of felt the
same size.

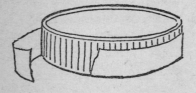

2 Glue some paper around
the edge of the lid.

3 Place the circles of foam
and felt on the lid and
cover them with a large
piece of felt.

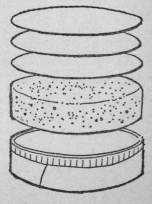

34

4 Cover the paper on the lid with fabric glue (not too thick) and, before it can dry, pull the edges of the large piece of felt around the lid, gathering them up below it. Smooth out any wrinkles around the edge of the lid and tie a string knot around the gathered felt. Press the felt well into the glued edge.

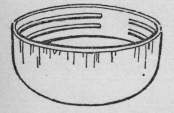

5 When the glue is dry, cut the excess felt away from the lid, leaving a neat edge. Make sure that any felt that is not firm is re-glued.

6 Glue braid around the base of the lid.

7 Having washed the label and glue off the coffee jar, glue the edge of a large piece of felt down it.

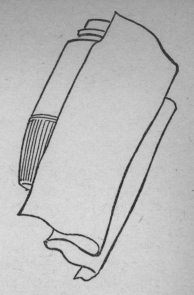

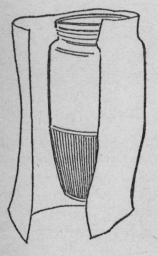

8 When the glue is dry, continue by stretching the felt around the jar, glueing a small bit at a time. Be careful not to use too much glue as it will show through the felt.

9 When completed, trim the felt, leaving a slight overlap.

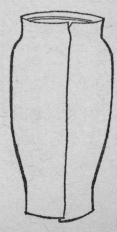

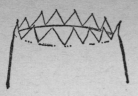

10 Cut the felt as shown and stretch each piece over the base, glueing each one in turn. Make sure that they do not overlap.

11 Glue a circle of felt over the base, and using a sharp knife, trim around the top of the jar just under where the lid fits.

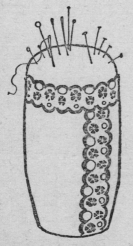

12 Stick a length of braid down the seam, making sure that it does not interfere with the lid.

Book ends

YOU WILL NEED
Scraps of wood
Wood glue
Wood screws
Sandpaper
Enamel paints

SPECIAL EQUIPMENT
A tenon saw
Set square or mitre block

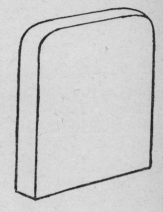

1 Cut four pieces of wood at least 12 mm (½ in) thick and about 10 cms (4 ins) wide into 12 cm (5 in) lengths.

2 Round off the corners of one end of each piece of wood. Sandpaper all the pieces smooth.

3 Attach the four pieces together, making two pairs. Use wood glue and countersunk screws, making sure that each pair is at right angles.

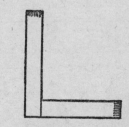

4 Cut up scraps of wood so that they are no longer than 12 cms (5 ins) and no shorter than 12 mms ($\frac{1}{2}$ in). The ends of the pieces of wood must be cut absolutely square, either by marking out with a set square or by cutting them on a mitre block.

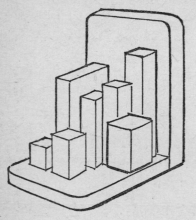

5 Sandpaper the pieces of wood and glue them in turn on to the book ends. They can form a pattern if you wish, but they could also be glued on in a random design.

6 Having made sure that all the wood is smooth and clean, paint the book ends with wood primer, followed by undercoat. The final coats of paint could be one colour or several, perhaps painting each block of wood a different colour.

Drink coasters

YOU WILL NEED
Scraps of perspex
Small pieces of felt
Wallpaper paste

SPECIAL EQUIPMENT
A file

1 Cut pieces of acrylic sheet (perspex) into 10 cm (4 in) squares, leaving the protective papers on both sides. Either suppliers of perspex will do this for you or you can do it by heavily scoring the perspex and snapping it, or you can saw it with a fine-toothed saw.

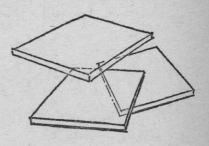

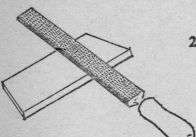

2 File the edges smooth and finish with sandpaper or wire wool.

3 Peel off the backing sheets and make sure that there is no dust on the perspex.

4 Decorate either by painting (with enamel paints) the underside of the coaster with a design, or by glueing a photograph face down on one side. Use wallpaper paste for glueing paper to perspex. Wipe all traces of paste away from any uncovered area with a damp cloth.

5 Paint the backs all over with enamel paint.

6 Glue the decorated perspex on to felt and, when dry, trim round the edges.

Kitchen rack

YOU WILL NEED
5 *small coffee jars*
Some scraps of wood
10 $\frac{1}{2}$-*in screws*
Paint or varnish
Sandpaper
Wood glue
Panel pins

SPECIAL EQUIPMENT
Fretsaw

1 Choose a piece of wood at least 12 mm ($\frac{1}{2}$ in) thick and 12 mm ($\frac{1}{2}$ in) wider than the diameter of the coffee jars. Cut this to length, allowing 12 mm ($\frac{1}{2}$ in) between each jar.

2 Cut a 8 cm (3 in) piece of plywood to the same length.

3 Draw a centre line through the plywood as shown and draw 25 cm (1 in) squares either side. Copy the pattern on to these squares.

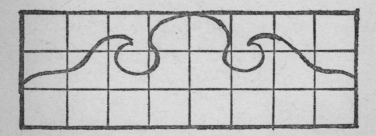

42

4 Cut out the shape with a fretsaw and sandpaper all the edges smooth.

5 Using glue and panel pins, attach the plywood to the other piece of wood and leave to dry.

6 Either varnish the assembly or decorate it using wood primer, undercoat and gloss paints.

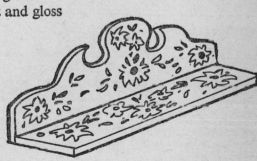

7 When dry, attach the lids to the underside of the assembly by piercing them with a nail and screwing them to the wood with two $\frac{1}{2}$-in screws in each lid.

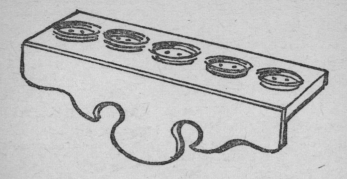

8 The coffee jars may be decorated on the outside with enamel paints.

Seed necklace

YOU WILL NEED
Seeds from one or two melons
Button thread

SPECIAL EQUIPMENT
None

1 Scoop the seeds from the melon and wash them in a fine sieve. Separate them from all the fibres and pulp.

2 Dry the seeds thoroughly in a warm place. String them on to the thread using a needle and thimble.

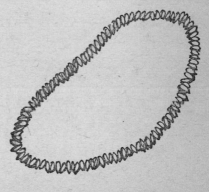

3 When the necklace is large enough, tie off the ends of the thread securely. The necklace may be tinted with cochineal, dyed or painted with a spray can.

Mighty Mouse

YOU WILL NEED
Closely-woven cloth
Scraps of felt
Short length of rope
Button thread
Stuffing (kapok or old pairs
  of tights)

SPECIAL EQUIPMENT
A sewing machine would be
useful

1 Cut out paper patterns to the measurements shown on the opposite page.

2 From your piece of cloth, cut out three sides and one back. From the felt cut out two ears and two eyes.

3 Seam two sides on to the back.

46

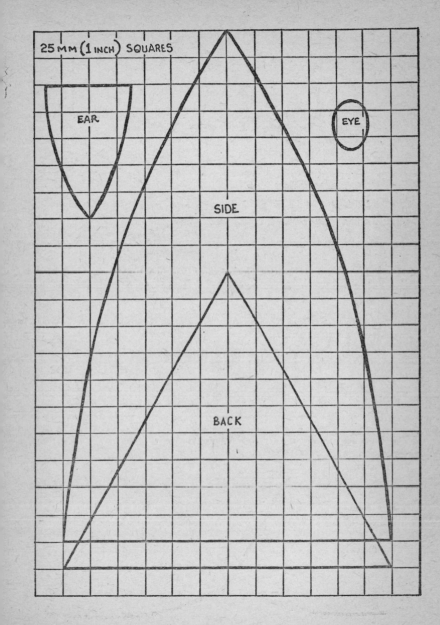

25 MM (1 INCH) SQUARES

EAR

EYE

SIDE

BACK

47

4 Seam the two sides together, leaving a small hole in the corner for the tail.

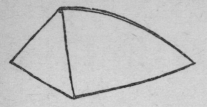

5 Seam the third side to the first two sides, leaving the end unsewn. Turn the assembly right side out.

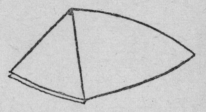

6 Pass the rope tail through the hole and sew it in place.

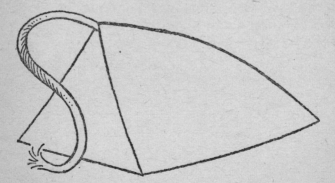

7 Stuff the mouse and sew up the remaining end seam.

8 Sew or glue the eyes in position and sew on the ears.

9 Attach a small piece of felt for the nose and attach button thread whiskers.

Piggy bank

YOU WILL NEED
A balloon
Some pieces of felt
Enamel paint
Wallpaper paste

SPECIAL EQUIPMENT
None

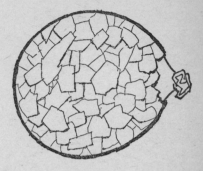

1 Partially blow up a balloon until it is about 13 cms (5 ins) in diameter. Stick small pieces of paper over it, using wallpaper paste, until five or six layers of paper have been built up. Leave the neck of the balloon uncovered.

2 When the paper is thoroughly dry, stick a small piece of Sellotape over the uncovered part of the neck. Pierce the balloon with a pin through the Sellotape. This will let the air escape slowly. Remove the balloon from the shell of paper.

3 Make the nose and legs by covering the ends of suitable bottles with baking foil and building up five layers of paper on each.

4 When the nose and legs are dry, remove them from the bottles and trim them with a pair of scissors.

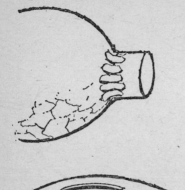

5 Attach the nose and legs by glueing small strips of paper between them and the body, again building up several layers.

6 Cut a slot in the top with a very sharp modelling knife so that a 50 pence piece will just go through.

7 Paint the pig with undercoat or emulsion followed by two coats of enamel. Further decorations may be applied with enamel.

8 Cut two ears and a tail out of felt and glue them into position.

Mosaic ashtray

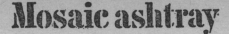

YOU WILL NEED
Card
Old stockings or tights
Polyfilla
Mosaic pieces or small flat shells
Scraps of felt

SPECIAL EQUIPMENT
None

Mosaic can usually be bought quite cheaply from good do-it-yourself shops.

1 Make a shallow tray about 10 cms (4 ins) square with card, Sellotaping the corners.

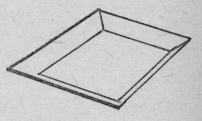

2 Cover the tray with kitchen foil.

3 Build up three layers of nylon stockings soaked in Polyfilla. Make the Polyfilla quite stiff or it will all flow to the bottom of the tray.

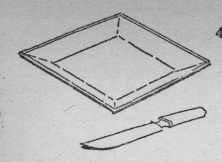

4 When dry, trim the top edge with a sharp knife and remove the ashtray from the card and foil.

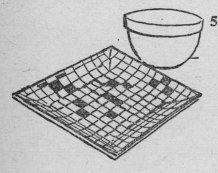

5 Set the mosaic into the top with more Polyfilla and, when dry, fill in the gaps, wiping off any excess with a damp cloth.

6 The base and sides may be sandpapered smooth and painted with enamel. Finally, glue a square of felt on to the base.

Flowerpot holder

YOU WILL NEED
Plastic flowerpot
Large bag of Polyfilla
Attractive pebbles or shells

SPECIAL EQUIPMENT
None

1 Stand the flowerpot upside down on a piece of scrap wood covered in kitchen foil. Mix up a thick paste of Polyfilla.

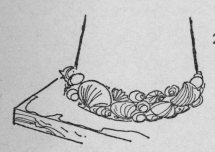

2 Attach the shells along the bottom of the flowerpot by embedding them in Polyfilla so that any gaps between the pebbles or shells are filled.

3 You will only be able to do one row at a time, otherwise the weight of Polyfilla and shells will make them all slide down the flowerpot. Wait until each row is going hard before starting the next.

4 Any excess Polyfilla may be scraped off before it is completely dry.

5 Continue building the rows until you reach the base of the flowerpot, but be careful that the decoration does not extend beyond this point.

6 The flowerpot holder can either be left as it is when you have finished scraping off the excess material, or it can be given one or two coats of polyurethane varnish.

String jar

1 Place the lid of a coffee jar over a block of wood and, using the flat end of the hammer, pierce a hole in the centre with the nail.

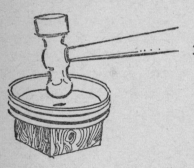

2 Turn the lid over and flatten the jagged edges of the hole with the rounded end of the hammer. Be careful not to close up the hole.

3 Wash the label and glue off the jar. The inside can be painted with enamel if desired. If this needs two coats, make sure that the first one is dry before applying the second.

4 Paint a base colour all over
the lid.

5 Decorate the jar and lid
with a design, using one
colour of enamel at a time,
and allowing each to dry
before starting the next.

6 When the paint is thoroughly
dry, thread the end of a
suitable ball of string
through the lid, place the
string in the jar, and replace
the lid.

Pressed flower picture

YOU WILL NEED
Freshly picked flowers
Stiff card
Art paper
A piece of glass
Glue
Blotting paper

SPECIAL EQUIPMENT
None

1 Remove any dead or loose petals or leaves from the flowers which you have chosen.

2 Arrange the flowers individually on a small sheet of blotting paper and cover it with another sheet of blotting paper. Place the flowers in their blotting paper between two thick pieces of wood.

3 The flowers must be pressed by placing a very heavy weight on the wood. A heavy piece of furniture is ideal. The flowers must now be left for at least two months to dry thoroughly.

4 Glue a piece of good quality coloured paper on to a piece of stiff card.

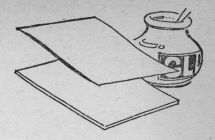

5 Arrange the flowers on the paper and glue them on individually. Be careful not to use too much glue. The glass will also help to hold them in place.

6 See page 92 for framing your flower arrangement.

Leaf skeleton

YOU WILL NEED
Some fresh leaves
A piece of blotting paper

SPECIAL EQUIPMENT
None

Leaf skeletons will look very good if they are incorporated in the pressed flower picture on the previous page.

1 Place a leaf on a piece of blotting paper.

2 Tap the leaf with a clothes brush. Do not tap too hard, or move the brush sideways.

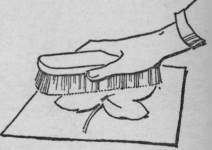

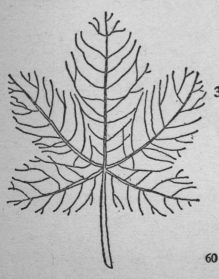

3 After a time the blotting paper will have absorbed all the thinner parts of the leaf, leaving the skeleton intact.

Two-tone flower

YOU WILL NEED
A flower with white petals,
*   such as a rose, carnation,*
*   or dahlia*
Coloured inks

SPECIAL EQUIPMENT
Two small test tubes

One of these flowers would make an excellent present by itself, or could be used when making the pressed flower picture on page 60.

1 Half fill the two test tubes with different coloured inks, and place them in a narrow glass.

2 Split the stem of the flower and place each half in either test tube.

3 In a short while the flower will change colour and can be removed. Bind the stem with cotton or raffia.

Christmas stocking

YOU WILL NEED
Felt for stocking
Other pieces of coloured felt
Trimming material such as
fur fabric, sequins and braid

SPECIAL EQUIPMENT
A sewing machine would be
useful

1 Cut out a paper pattern to
the drawing shown on the
opposite page, and from it
cut out two pieces of felt.

2 Decorate one of the pieces
of felt by sewing on scraps
of felt, braid, sequins and
anything else that is available.
Do not let the decoration
go too close to the edge.

3 Sew the two halves together,
and either go around the
edge with pinking shears or
turn the stocking inside out.
Remember which side of
the material the decoration
must be before starting.

4 Sew a felt loop at the top
and trim the top with
braid or fur fabric.

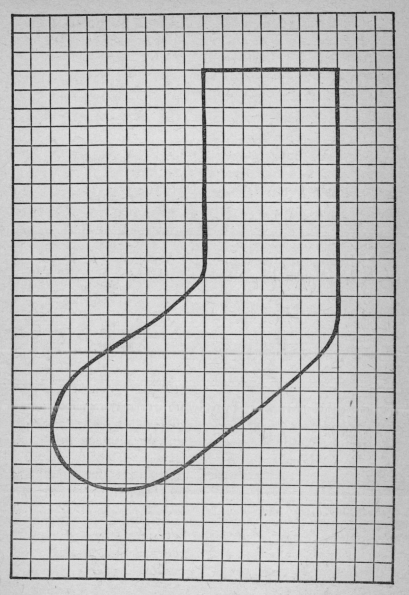

Photograph lampshade

YOU WILL NEED
Lampshade frame
Cloth tape
Braid
Photographs
Art paper

SPECIAL EQUIPMENT
None

1 Cover the rings and upright bars of a lampshade frame by wrapping them tightly round with cloth tape. Sew the ends to keep the binding firm.

2 Lay the frame on a sheet of good quality, thick art paper. Roll the frame over the paper one complete turn, marking the ends as you go.

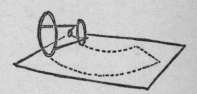

3 Cut out the paper shape, allowing a small overlap at the join, and make sure it fits the frame.

4 Cut holes in the paper slightly smaller than the photographs that you have chosen.

5 Glue the photographs very firmly into position.

6 Braid can be glued round each photograph if you wish.

7 Attach the paper to the frame by very gently sewing the paper to the binding. Also glue the overlap.

8 Glue or sew braid around the top and bottom and also down the seam if desired.

Decorated wooden spoon

YOU WILL NEED
New wooden spoon
Sandpaper
Undercoat
Various colours enamel paint
Coloured ribbon

SPECIAL EQUIPMENT
Drill with small bit

A decorated wooden spoon makes an attractive kitchen ornament.

1 Drill a hole in the end of the spoon and thoroughly sandpaper the spoon all over.

2 Apply a coat of undercoat and leave to dry before painting the spoon with a base colour of enamel.

3 Decorate the spoon with any design you wish, using one colour of enamel at a time, and allowing each colour to dry.

4 Make a bow for the top of the spoon, also a loop so that it can be hung up.

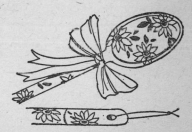

Memo pad

YOU WILL NEED
A piece of Formica
A small piece of felt
Enamel paint
A felt-tipped pen

SPECIAL EQUIPMENT
Metal ruler
File

1 Cut out a piece of white Formica 18 cms (7 ins) × 12 cms (5 ins). Formica is cut by scoring the face with a sharp knife against a straight edge and putting it face down over the edge of a table and snapping it. Many suppliers will do this for you.

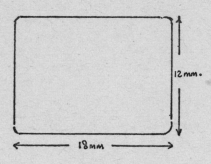

2 With a file and sandpaper, smooth the edges and round off the corners.

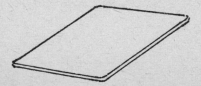

3 Wrap and glue a strip of
felt around the cap of a
felt-tipped pen.

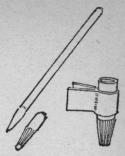

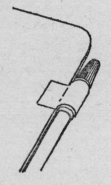

4 Glue the ends of the strip
to the back of the Formica
as shown.

5 Using enamel paint, write
the word "MEMO" across
the top. You can use the
memo pad again and again,
wiping it clean each time
with a damp cloth.

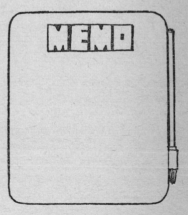

Tie and dye scarf

YOU WILL NEED
A remnant of white cotton
60 cms (2 ft) square
Some cold water dyes

SPECIAL EQUIPMENT
None

1 Find a smooth round pebble and tie it into the centre of the cotton square.

2 Bind string *very tightly* under the pebble and continue to tie further tight bindings along the material.

3 More stones can be added in the binding if you want. The bindings can also be varied by individually tying the four corners of the square.

4 Another method of preparation is to rub wax thoroughly into the material before dyeing. The wax can be removed when the scarf is dry by ironing the cloth through a piece of blotting paper.

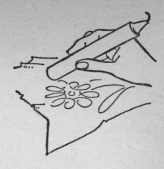

5 Follow the instructions on the dye packets very carefully and be careful not to stain your hands or your clothes. If you have not done dyeing before you should ask an adult to help.

6 Undo all the bindings and allow the material to dry. Repeat the process with another colour if you wish. Hem the cloth with a small turning all round.

Stocking flowers

YOU WILL NEED
*A few old pairs of tights or
  stockings*
A selection of dyes
Some wire
Raffia

SPECIAL EQUIPMENT
Wire cutters

1 Following the instructions
  on the packets carefully, dye
  some old tights different
  colours. If you have not
  dyed anything before, ask
  an adult to help you.

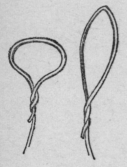

2 Bend some pieces of wire
  into the shapes of petals
  and leaves and twist the
  stems together.

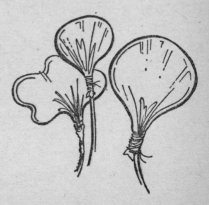

3 Stretch a piece of stocking
  over each wire loop and
  bind the stem with cotton.

4 Group the petals and leaves
into flowers and bend them
as required. Bind all the
stems together, using raffia.

5 The individual flowers may be arranged together in a vase.

Modern vase

YOU WILL NEED
Odd lengths of plastic piping
Plastic bottles
Polystyrene cement

SPECIAL EQUIPMENT
Hacksaw

1 Obtain some odd lengths of plastic piping. A plumber will probably have some scrap pieces. Select some plastic bottles that will just fit inside these pipes.

2 Cut the pipes with a hacksaw and sandpaper the ends smooth.

3 Cut the top off each plastic bottle so that it comes just below the top of each pipe.

4 Glue the pipes together with polystyrene cement.

5 Paint the pipe assembly with enamel paint.

6 The vase assembly should be placed on a flat surface. Fill the bottles with water and flowers and lower them into place.

Flowerpot tray

YOU WILL NEED

Some wood 15 *cms* (6 *ins*) ×
   1 *metre* (3 *ft*)
Some other scraps of wood
Wood glue
Wood screws

SPECIAL EQUIPMENT
Tenon saw

1 Cut two lengths of wood
45 cms (18 ins) long ×
15 cms (6 ins) wide and at
least 12 mm (½ in) thick.
These are the two uprights.

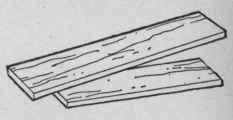

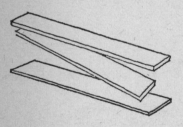

2 Cut two more pieces out of
scrap 45 cms (18 ins) long ×
10 cms (4 ins) wide and at
least 12 mm (½ in) thick
for the sides. Cut also a
piece of thin plywood or
hardboard 12 cms (5 ins)
wide × 45 cms (18 ins)
long for the base.

3 Lightly attach the plywood base to the sides with panel
pins. These pins should only be knocked half way in at
this stage.

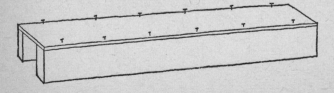

4 Attach the sides to each upright, using wood screws and glue. The sides should slope slightly inwards, as shown.

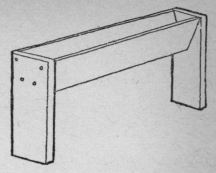

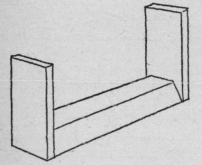

5 Remove the base and re-fix it to the sides using wood glue and screws.

6 Starting with wood primer, paint the assembly with enamel paint.

Jar of bath salts

YOU WILL NEED
Washing soda
Poster paint
Large jar
Ribbon
Enamel paints

SPECIAL EQUIPMENT
None

1 Fill a polythene bag with enough soda crystals to fill the jar.

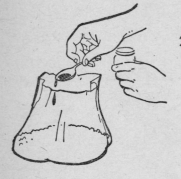

2 Pour a very small amount of poster paint into the bag and shake it all up together. Any large lumps may be crushed with a rolling pin.

3 Decorate the jar by painting it with enamel paint.

4 Tie a ribbon bow around the top of the jar.

5 Having made sure that all the poster paint has been absorbed by the soda, pour the bath salts into the jar.

Topsy turvy doll

YOU WILL NEED
Scraps of material
Kapok or similar stuffing

SPECIAL EQUIPMENT
A sewing machine would be useful

This rag doll is two dolls in one. The skirt is double-sided and completely covers either half of the doll.

1 Cut out four pieces of flesh-coloured material as shown.

2 Placing right sides together, sew them together in pairs to form the bodies, leaving an opening in each of the two wider ends.

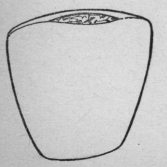

3 Turn the bodies right side out and fill them with stuffing.

4 To make the heads, roll up balls of stuffing to the required size and cover them by draping a circle of material over each and gathering round to form the neck.

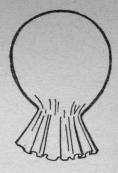

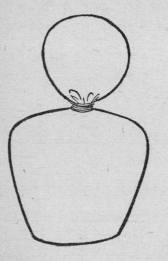

5 Bind each neck with cotton and insert the loose material of the neck into the hole of each body. Sew the heads into place, closing off the gap in the top of each body.

6 Make four arms by cutting out eight pieces of material. Placing right sides together, sew all round except for the tops. Turn the arms right side out and fill them with stuffing.

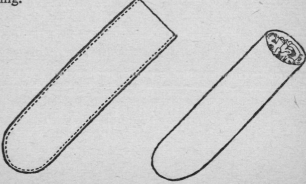

7 Sew the arms into place so that each arm falls either way, and sew the two bodies together.

8 The features on the face can either be embroidered on or buttons can be attached for eyes, etc.

9 Sew on wool for the hair.

10 When making the clothes, make sure that the double-sided skirt is long enough to completely hide one side of the doll.

Letter rack

YOU WILL NEED
Scraps of wood
Wood glue
Panel pins
Old postage stamps
Wallpaper paste

SPECIAL EQUIPMENT
Fretsaw

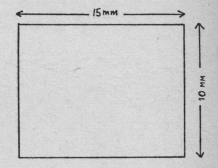

1 Cut out a piece of plywood
15 cms (6 ins) × 10 cms
(4 ins).

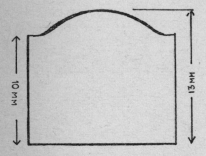

2 Cut out another piece 15 cms
(6 ins) × 13 cms (5 ins) and
shape the top with a fretsaw
as shown.

3 Cut two lengths of wood
10 cms (4 ins) long. They
should be 3 cms (1 in) wide
and 1 cm ($\frac{1}{2}$ in) thick.

4 Join all four pieces together as shown with panel pins and glue.

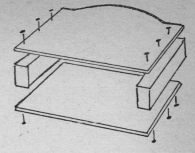

5 Cut a piece of plywood 18 cms (7 ins) × 6 cms (2½ ins) and, using panel pins and glue, attach this base to the assembly as shown.

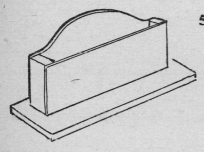

6 Smooth the letter rack with sandpaper, rounding off all the corners.

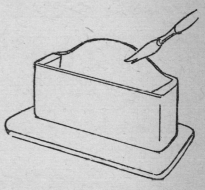

7 Paint the letter rack with one coat of wood primer and one coat of undercoat.

8 Soak postage stamps off old letters and paste them all over the wood. When the glue is completely dry, apply two coats of polyurethane varnish over the stamps.

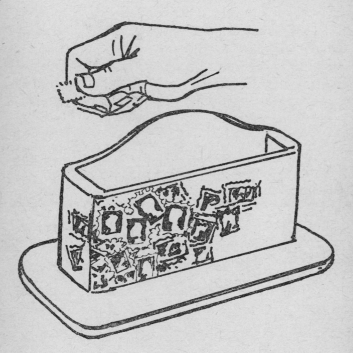

Jigsaw puzzle

YOU WILL NEED
A picture
A piece of good quality card
Wallpaper paste

SPECIAL EQUIPMENT
A steel ruler or straight edge
A sharp knife
An old piece of hardboard or plywood

1 Paste the picture on to a piece of slightly larger card. Make sure you smooth out all the wrinkles, working from the centre to the edge. Leave this to dry for at least two days. Place weights on it to make sure that it does not bend.

2 Using the straight edge and knife, trim the edges of the picture. Place an old piece of hardboard under the picture to prevent the knife from damaging the table.

3 Using straight cuts, cut the picture into as many pieces as you wish. It could be nicely presented in a flat, painted tin with the name of the jigsaw on the lid.

THE LITTLE FISHERMAN

Spectacle case

SPECIAL EQUIPMENT
*A sewing machine would be
useful*

1 Cut out four pieces of
material 8 cms (3½ ins) ×
17 cms (7 ins).

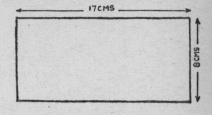

2 Divide the four pieces into
pairs so that each pair
consists of a lining and an
outer. One of the outers can
be decorated by embroidery
or by attaching felt shapes
to it.

3 Seam each pair right sides
together, leaving one short
end open.

4 Turn each pair inside out, and sew up the short ends.

5 Oversew the two halves together with embroidery silk or wool, making the stitching as even as possible. Do not sew all the way up the sides.

Framing photographs

YOU WILL NEED
Card and paper
Coloured sticky tape or braid
Paper glue
Glass cut to size

SPECIAL EQUIPMENT
None

1 Glue the photograph to a
piece of white card, leaving
a border all the way round.
Make sure that it is straight
and glued down everywhere.

2 Cut a piece of paper to the
same size as the card and,
using a knife and straight
edge, cut a piece out of the
middle slightly smaller than
the photograph. Some very
attractive papers can be
bought cheaply at an art
shop. A border can be
drawn around the photograph
with a ruler. This will give
the framing that professional
look.

3 A piece of glass must be bought the same size as the card backing. Please remember that glass is very sharp and should only be handled whilst one is wearing old gloves.

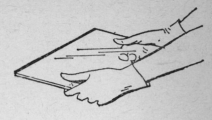

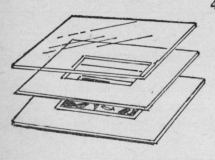

4 Clean the glass thoroughly (especially the surface which will be against the picture), then place the backing card with photograph, the paper, and the glass together and hold them in place on three sides with little pieces of Sellotape.

5 On the fourth side, bind the edge with coloured sticky tape. Remove one piece of Sellotape at a time before binding each edge. The tape must completely seal the edges and be turned down over the front and back, making neat corners.

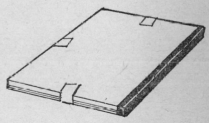

6 If you are unable to get any coloured tape, use Sellotape, and finish off the edges by glueing braid over them.

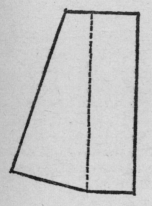

7 Make a stand for the frame by cutting out a piece of thick card as shown and scoring down the centre line. Glue this on to the back, and when dry bend the leg out at right angles to the picture.

Plant trainer

YOU WILL NEED
A few plant-training sticks
Fuse wire

SPECIAL EQUIPMENT
None

*Any gardening enthusiast will find this a useful gadget
for training young plants in flowerpots.*

1 Lay out the sticks as shown,
making sure that the two
vertical pieces are close
enough to go into a
medium-sized flowerpot.

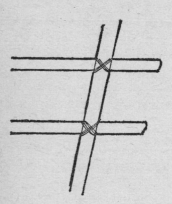

2 Join the sticks together by
criss-cross binding with the
fuse wire.

3 Paint the plant trainer with
enamel paints.

Electrical kit

YOU WILL NEED
Useful electrical tools
Thick cloth
Cloth tape

SPECIAL EQUIPMENT
A sewing machine would be useful

This kit can be as large or as small as you like. Here are some suggestions: Neon screwdriver, pencil torch, wire cutters, fuse wire, cartridge fuses, pointed-nose pliers, insulating tape – and how about including a couple of flex shorteners that you can find on page 118?

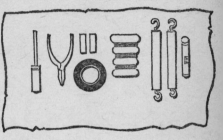

1 Lay out all the items on a cloth, in such a way that if they were held firm the cloth could be rolled up.

2 Mark the position of each item and trim the cloth around them, leaving room for a hem.

3 Hem the edges of the cloth.

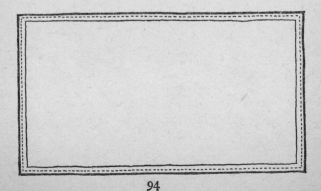

4 Make pockets out of cloth or ribbon and sew them in place so that each item is held firm.

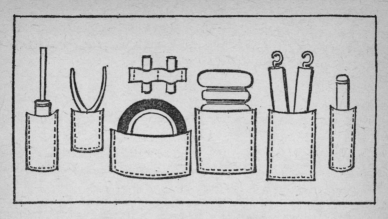

5 Sew a long tape by its centre to the middle of one edge, as shown. The tool roll can then be tied up.

Laundry bag

YOU WILL NEED
Some heavy cloth material
A wooden coat hanger

SPECIAL EQUIPMENT
A sewing machine would be useful

Hang this bag on a bedroom or dressing-room wall or door for collecting laundry.

1 Cut out two squares of material. The length of each side should be slightly greater than the width of a coat hanger. The top edges should be slightly curved.

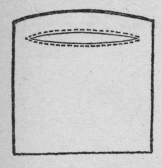

2 Cut a slot near the curved edge of one piece and hem round it.

3 Decorate the piece which has been slotted with embroidery or collage.

4 Join the two halves together, making sure that the decorated side is facing inwards. Leave a very small gap in the centre of the top edge.

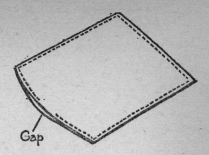

Gap

5 Turn the material right side out (through the slot) and insert a wooden coat hanger into the top.

Laundry

Milk sign

YOU WILL NEED
Plywood
Small screw
Small washer
Enamel paints

SPECIAL EQUIPMENT
Fretsaw

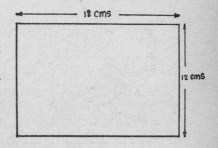

18 cms

12 cms

1 Cut out a piece of wood
18 cms (7 ins) × 12 cms
(5 ins). Sandpaper it smooth
all over.

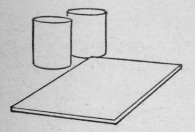

2 Paint the plywood with
wood primer followed by
two coats of undercoat,
leaving each coat to dry
before applying the next.

3 With a fretsaw, cut out the tail to the pattern shown and
paint it as described above.

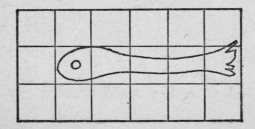

1 cm squares

4 Draw 1 cm squares on to the painted plywood and copy the design. Paint it with enamel. Also paint the tail.

5 Attach the tail to the cow with the screw, using the washer to separate them.

Table mats....

YOU WILL NEED
Soft rope
Stiff card
Felt

SPECIAL EQUIPMENT
None

1 Coil a long length of rope in a circle and stitch it together on one side only. When the coil is large enough, sew the end over as neatly as possible.

2 Cut a circle of stiff card, the same size as the finished coil, and glue a piece of felt on to one side, stretching the felt as it is glued.

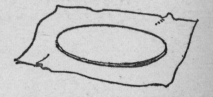

3 Cut the felt in a circle about 25 mm (1 in) from the edge of the card and stretch it over the edge, glueing it into position.

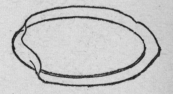

4 Glue the stitched side of the rope coil to the card.

...with matching napkin rings

YOU WILL NEED
Soft rope

SPECIAL EQUIPMENT
None

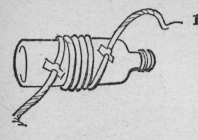

1 Wrap a length of rope four times around a bottle of a suitable diameter. Leave the ends fairly long and secure them with sticky tape.

2 Sew the four coils of rope firmly together and remove the ring from the bottle.

3 Turn the ring inside out so that the stitching is now on the inside and tie a reef knot (right over left, and left over right) with the two free ends.

4 Sew the two ends of the knot inside the ring as neatly as possible, cutting off any spare rope.

Tissue box cover

YOU WILL NEED
Thin, stretchy material
Thin elastic
Braid
A box of tissues

SPECIAL EQUIPMENT
A sewing machine would be
useful

1 Lay the tissue box upside down in the middle of the reverse side of the cloth and mark around it with a felt-tipped pen.

2 Rock the box on to each side and each end, marking round each side as you do this.

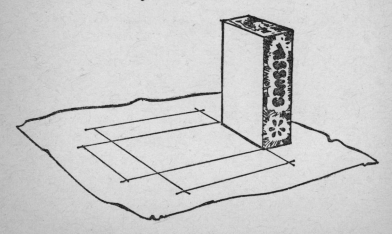

3 Add 25 mm (1 in) to each end and cut out the material.

4 Cut out a slot in the centre of the material large enough to allow the tissues to come through, and turn the edges of it neatly.

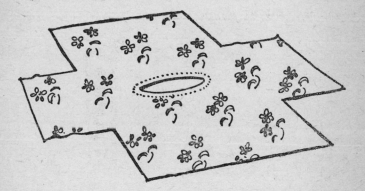

5 Trim the edges of the slot with braid.

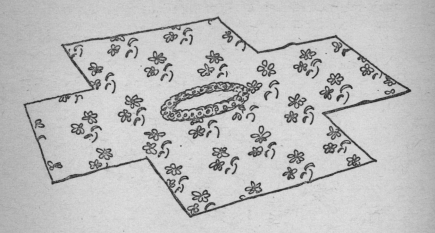

6 Seam the four corners, making the seams as small as possible.

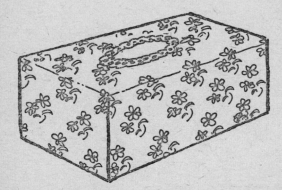

7 Make a turning all the way around the edges of the material, wide enough to allow the elastic to go through. Leave one corner open.

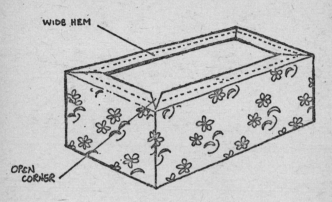

WIDE HEM

OPEN CORNER

8 Attach one end of the elastic to a small safety pin and thread it through the hem. Sew the elastic together at the open corner so that the cover will fit the box snugly.

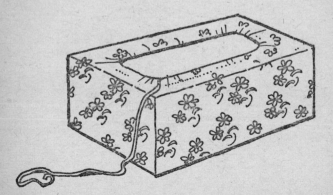

Jewellery tree

YOU WILL NEED
Stiff wire
Absorbent cloth rags·
Plaster of Paris
Scrap of hardboard
Fuse wire

SPECIAL EQUIPMENT
Pliers
Wire cutters

This jewellery tree can be stood on a dressing-table and is a very useful ornament on which to hang odd pieces of jewellery.

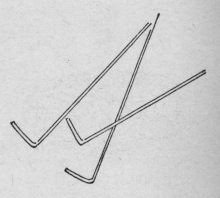

1 Cut about 36 lengths of wire 35 cms (14 ins) long and bend each one at right angles about 5 cms (2 ins) from one end.

2 Bundle all the wires together so that the bent ends splay out in a circle. Bind the wires for about 10 cms (4 ins) up the stem with the fuse wire.

106

3 The bundle of wires must now be divided branch by branch and bound with fuse wire. Begin by dividing the main stem in two, and then each of those into a further two, etc. Trim the branches as required with the wire cutters.

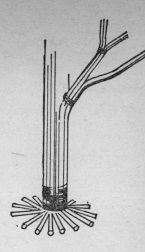

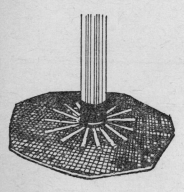

4 Cut a piece of hardboard in an irregular shape. The "roots" of the tree must not project over the edge. Stand the tree on the rough side of the hardboard.

5 Cut strips of cloth about 1 cm (½ in) wide, and dip them in a bowl of Plaster of Paris. The plaster should be the consistency of cream. Wrap the strips around the trunk and branches and also over the roots. Build up the layers until the right thickness is achieved. The plaster can also be carved when dry to form the bark.

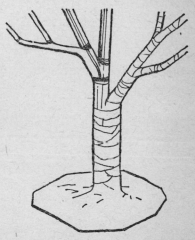

6 Paint the tree with enamel paints. Most model shops can supply matting agent which, when mixed with the paint, produces a dull finish.

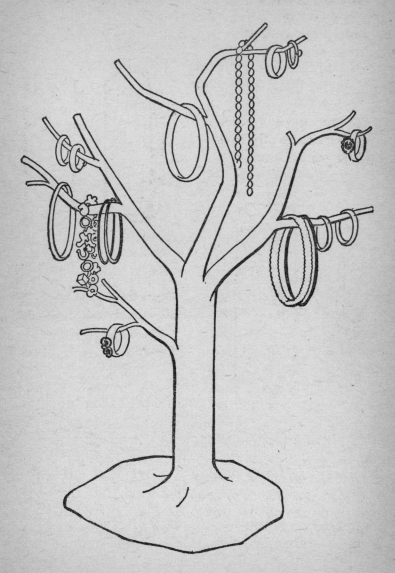

Decorated clothes-brush

YOU WILL NEED
A clothes-brush
Sewing odds and ends

SPECIAL EQUIPMENT
None

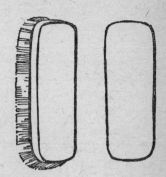

1 Cut out a piece of material the same size as the back of the clothes-brush.

2 Decorate the material with either embroidery, felt or collage, or by sewing on buttons.

3 Glue the decorated material in place and glue on a length of braid or ribbon around the edge.

Hanging basket

YOU WILL NEED
22 *straight twigs*
Wood preservative (*Creosote*)
Scrap wood
Metal ring
Thin nylon rope

SPECIAL EQUIPMENT
A drill

A hanging basket can be lined with moss and planted with suitable flowers, such as geraniums.

1 Cut 22 straight twigs 25 cms (10 ins) long. Make sure that they are dry but not brittle.

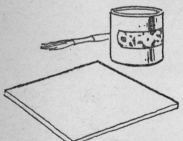

2 Cut a piece of plywood 25 cms (10 ins) square and coat it with a wood preservative such as Creosote.

3 Drill a hole slightly larger than the diameter of the rope in both ends of each twig about 25 mm (1 in) in from the end. This measurement need not be exact as long as the holes have the same distance between them on each twig.

4 The plywood must also have a hole drilled in each corner which will correspond to the holes in the twigs.

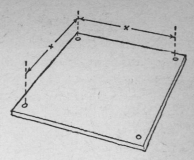

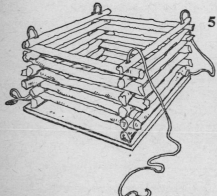

5 Tie a knot in one end of each of four lengths of rope. Thread the ropes up through the base and begin threading each twig on to the ropes as shown.

6 Tie the ropes off on to the metal ring.

Felt slippers

YOU WILL NEED
Pieces of felt
Pieces of foam
  1 cm (½ in) thick
Card
Fabric glue

SPECIAL EQUIPMENT
A sewing machine would be useful

1 Ask the person who will wear the slippers to place one foot on a piece of card so that you can draw around it. (Otherwise borrow one of their shoes.) Then cut out two pieces of card to that shape.

2 Also cut out two pieces of foam the same shape.

3 Place one of the pieces of card on the felt, mark round, and cut out four pieces of felt, leaving an extra 5 mm (¼ in) border all round. Cut out two more pieces of felt exactly the same size as the card.

4 Place each pair of felt shapes together and sew together along the line, leaving the toe end open. Turn them right side out.

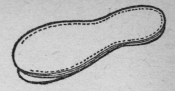

5 Put the foam and card into each slipper and sew up the toes neatly.

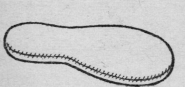

6 Cut out two strips of felt 6 cms (2 ins) wide and at least 18 cms (7 ins) long. (If you choose to use another type of material, the edges must be hemmed.)

7 Stand on each slipper and put the strips of material over each foot. Cut them to length so that they project under the slipper by about 1 cm ($\frac{1}{2}$ in).

8 Attach these strips to the underneath of each slipper with stitches or glue. They may be decorated with embroidery or by glueing on felt shapes.

9 Finally, glue the two spare pieces of felt on to the underside of each slipper.

Flex shortener

YOU WILL NEED
2 screw hooks
A piece of dowelling

SPECIAL EQUIPMENT
Bradawl

This is a very handy gadget for keeping long flexes tidy.

1 Cut a piece of 12 mm ($\frac{1}{2}$ in) dowel 8 cms (3 ins) long and smooth the ends with sandpaper.

2 With the bradawl (or other pointed implement), make a small hole in both ends and screw in the two screw hooks.

3 The flex shortener is used by wrapping the flex around the dowel and securing it at either end with the two screw hooks.

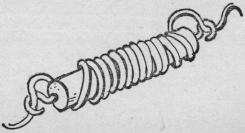

Putting a name to it

YOU WILL NEED
*A very good quality artist's
brush
Good quality enamel paint*

SPECIAL EQUIPMENT
None

*Sign writing is a skilful art, but it is quite possible for
anyone to achieve good results with a little practice.
Follow these instructions carefully.*

1 Choose some lettering from
a magazine and make sure
that the letters of the word
that you want to write all
appear in the same style of
type.

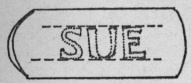

2 Draw two lines on the
object that you are going
to paint and carefully copy
the letters on to it in pencil.

3 Dip your brush into the well-stirred paint and practise
painting straight lines with a single pass of the brush. If the
line is not even, don't fiddle at it with the edge of the brush,
it will only make matters worse. Lay the brush nearly flat
along the line, where possible with the handle pointing in
the direction of the line.

Here are some suggestions of things that you could paint a name on.

Glove puppet

YOU WILL NEED
Wallpaper paste
Scraps of material
Poster paints
Brown sticky tape

SPECIAL EQUIPMENT
A sewing machine would be useful

1 Make a tube of thin cardboard about 3 cms (1½ ins)
long, wide enough to fit
easily over a finger.

2 Roll up a ball of newspaper
and attach it to the tube by
criss-crossing strips of
brown tape over it. This
will become the head and
neck of the puppet.

3 Build up the features by
glueing on very small pieces
of newspaper. The smaller
the pieces, the better the
end result.

4 Build up a small ridge
around the base of the neck.

5 Paint the face with poster
paints.

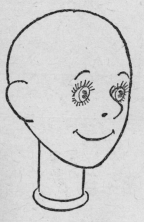

6 Glue pieces of wool in place
for the hair.

7 Cut out two pieces of cloth to the pattern and sew them right sides together. Leave the top unsewn.

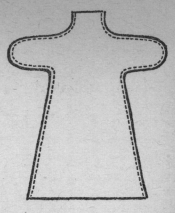

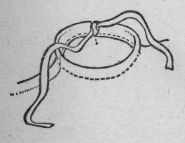

8 Turn the body right side out. Make a turning at the top and thread a piece of ribbon tape through it.

9 Hem the bottom of the dress. The costume can be built up in any way you wish. Fix the costume to the head by pulling the ribbon right over the neck ridge and tying it securely.

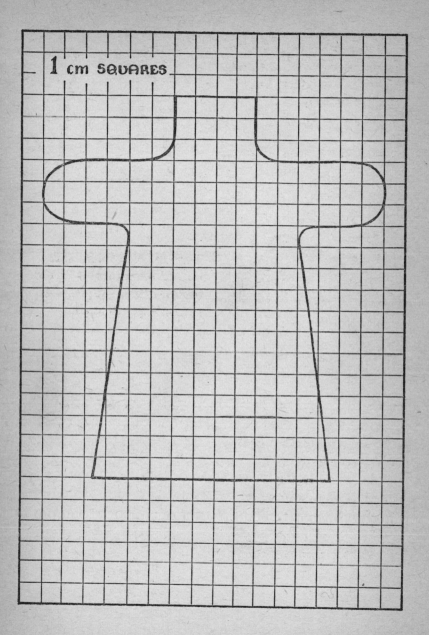

1 cm SQUARES

Coat hanger

YOU WILL NEED
A piece of 12 mm ($\frac{1}{2}$ in)
thick plywood
Enamel paints

SPECIAL EQUIPMENT
Tenon saw
Bradawl

1 Cut a piece of plywood as shown and sandpaper smooth.

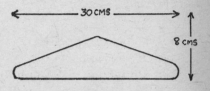

2 Bore a small hole in the top and screw in a hook from an old wooden coat hanger.

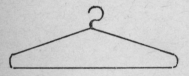

3 Paint the wood with wood primer and gloss paint. Copy the design shown on to one side. Paint the design with enamel paints.

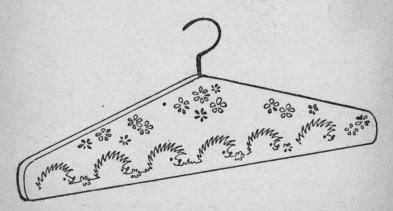

Sweet jar soldier

YOU WILL NEED
Wallpaper paste
Enamel paints

SPECIAL EQUIPMENT
A sharp knife

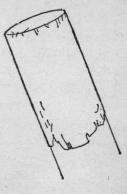

1 Cover the bottom of a washing-up liquid bottle with aluminium cooking foil.

2 Paste at least five layers of newspaper over the foil. The pieces of newspaper should be no more than 2 cms (¾ in) square.

3 When you have finished pasting on the newspaper, let the whole thing dry and remove it from the bottle. Peel the foil away from the inside.

4 Repeat the whole process so that you end up with two papier maché jars. One of these will be the lid and the other the base.

5 When you have decided on the overall height that the soldier should be, cut the two jars accurately so that you have a lid which is his head and a base which is his body. Make sure that these fit well together.

6 Cut a strip of card and glue it round the inside of the base so that about 1 cm ($\frac{3}{8}$ in) projects over the top. To make sure that the edges of the papier maché do not fray, smooth them over with paste.

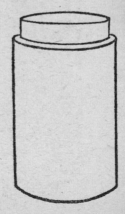

7 Give the two halves a coat of wood primer or white emulsion and allow to dry.

8 Draw the soldier on to the jar in pencil and paint him with enamel paints.

100 Games For One Player

BY J. B. PICK

Alone? Bored? Nothing to do?
Never again!

Find a whole new world of games in this exciting collection
of good ideas, which will keep you happy whenever you're
on your own.

Have you ever played Drippy Steps, One-Man Fives,
Peculiar Things, Bottle Music or Taboo?

There are outdoor games, indoor games, ball games, table
games, pencil and paper games, eye games and listening
games, games to play in your head – and dozens of en-
thralling Patience games.

All to help you enjoy the luxury of being by yourself.

Publication: December 1974. Price: 30p

Armada

Armada Ghost Stories

Have you ever felt a ghostly 'presence' in an empty room, or seen a shadowy figure standing by your bed?

Dip into one of Armada's hair-raising collections of ghostly happenings and feel those icy shivers run down your spine!

The First Armada Book of True Ghost Stories

EDITED BY CHRISTINE BERNARD

Dare you enter the unknown world of spirits in these startling tales – all chillingly true? Read about the amazing Talking Mongoose, the despairing Man in the Iron Cage, and the dreadful curse on the Emperor's motor car. And study photographs of real ghosts!

Publication: December 1974 Price: 30p

Armada Ghost Books Nos. 1 - 6

EDITORS: CHRISTINE BERNARD AND MARY DANBY

Spine-chilling stories of spectres and hauntings by the score. Ghosts of all kinds – weird ones, wicked one, frightening ones – even friendly ones! Collect them all – if you dare . . .

Armada

Armada

Armada books are chosen by children all over the world. They're designed to fit your pocket, and your pocket money too – why not build up your own Armada library? There are hundreds of exciting titles and favourite series to collect, and their bright spines look marvellous on any bookshelf. Armada have something for everyone:

Books by popular authors like **Enid Blyton** – **Malcolm Saville** – **Elinor Brent-Dyer** – **Alfred Hitchcock**, etc.

The best mysteries and most exciting adventure stories.

Favourite characters like **Jennings** – **William** – **Nancy Drew** – **The Hardy Boys** – **Biggles** – **The Three Investigators** – **The Lone Piners** – and many, many more.

Pony books by the Pullein-Thompson sisters, Mary Gervaise and Judith Berrisford.

A wonderful collection of famous children's stories.

Ghost books to make your hair stand on end!

A terrific collection of **quiz, puzzle** and **fun books to** entertain you for hours.

These are just a few of the good things Armada has in store for you.

If you'd like a complete up-to-date list of Armada books, send a stamped, addressed envelope to:
Armada Books,
14 St James's Place,
London SW1